0/1719L

The Art of the Piano

Volume 1

Masterful Sacred Solos by Mark Hayes

Level Descriptions

Level 1: Easy to moderately easy rhythmically and in technical demands; hands mostly in the middle of the keyboard

Level 2: Intermediate to moderate difficulty with a variety of musical styles; expanded range and more rhythmically demanding

Level 3: Advanced musically and in technical demands; use of full keyboard, scale and arpeggio passages, and stylistically demanding

Lorenz
www.lorenz.com

Editor: Larry Shackey
Music Engraving: Linda Taylor
Cover Design: Jeff Richards
ISBN: 978-1-4291-1543-8

Foreword

When I studied piano at Baylor University, I learned the importance of artful playing…such things as projecting the melody above other notes in a passage, how to shape a melodic phrase, and the nuances of pedaling, timing, and dynamics. Even though I don't play classical music on a regular basis anymore, I still try to play artfully, whatever I am playing. Certainly the music I play in a concert or for worship deserves my best effort so that it fully reflects the glory of God.

The Art of the Piano is a new series of high-caliber and advanced piano solos that will call you to play with artistry…to let your natural gifts shine through so that God is glorified. These solos can be played in worship, in concert, and in contests if you choose. Some have a distinct classical personality; some contain jazz idioms and lush harmonies. When I arrange for piano, I imagine I am writing for an orchestra. Feel the drama and spirit of my arrangements and let your emotions speak through your fingers.

In the future, I will be adding new volumes to this series such as *The Art of the Piano: Christmas* and *The Art of the Piano: Jazz*. I look forward to hearing from you if you have suggestions.

I delight in providing creative solos for you to use in ministry. May these arrangements resonate deep within you and provide hours of inspiration for you and others.

—*Mark Hayes*

Contents

Come, Christians, Join to Sing

Mark Hayes
Tune: **MADRID**
by Christian H. Bateman, 1813-1889

Stately ♩ = 120

Duration: 3:10

70/1719L-3

Morning Has Broken

Mark Hayes
Tune: BUNESSAN
Traditional Gaelic Melody

Duration: 4:00

10

70/1719L-10

for Joan Bandy

All Hail the Power of Jesus' Name

DIADEM, MILES LANE and CORONATION

Mark Hayes

Duration: 3:35

DIADEM, by James Ellor (1819-1899)

*MILES LANE, by William Shrubsole (1760-1806)

*CORONATION, *by Oliver Holden (1765-1844)

for Kathy Beck

And Can It Be

Mark Hayes

Tune: SAGINA
by Thomas Campbell, 1777-1844

Stately ♩ = 104

Duration: 3:20

70/1719L-21

My Jesus, I Love Thee

Mark Hayes
Tune: **GORDON**
by Adoniram J. Gordon, 1838-1895

Duration: 3:50

for Becki Slagle Mayo

All Creatures of Our God and King

Mark Hayes

Tune: **LASST UNS ERFREUEN**
Geistliche Kirchengesänge, 1623

Duration: 2:55

www.lorenz.com

for Shelley Dennis

Battle Hymn of the Republic

Mark Hayes
Tune: **BATTLE HYMN**
American Folk Song, 19th century

Duration: 4:00

70/1719L-36

Jesus Is All the World to Me

Mark Hayes
Tune: **ELIZABETH**
by Will L. Thompson 1847-1909

Duration: 2:40

Go Down, Moses

Mark Hayes
Traditional spiritual

Duration: 2:45

for Ann Waite

He Leadeth Me! O Blessed Thought

Mark Hayes
Tune: **HE LEADETH ME**
by William B. Bradbury, 1816-1868

Slowly, with freedom ♩ = 72

mf

poco accel.

rit.

Slightly faster ♩ = 76

bring out melody

mp *a tempo*

Duration: 4:00